AF201335

Impressum
Verlag: BABADADA GmbH, Nedderfeld 112 , 22529 Hamburg
Geschäftsführer / Verlagsleitung: Harald Hof
Druck: Books on Demand GmbH, In de Tarpen 42, 22848 Norderstedt

Imprint
Publisher: BABADADA GmbH, Nedderfeld 112 , 22529 Hamburg, Germany
Managing Director / Publishing direction: Harald Hof
Print: Books on Demand GmbH, In de Tarpen 42, 22848 Norderstedt

school

colegio

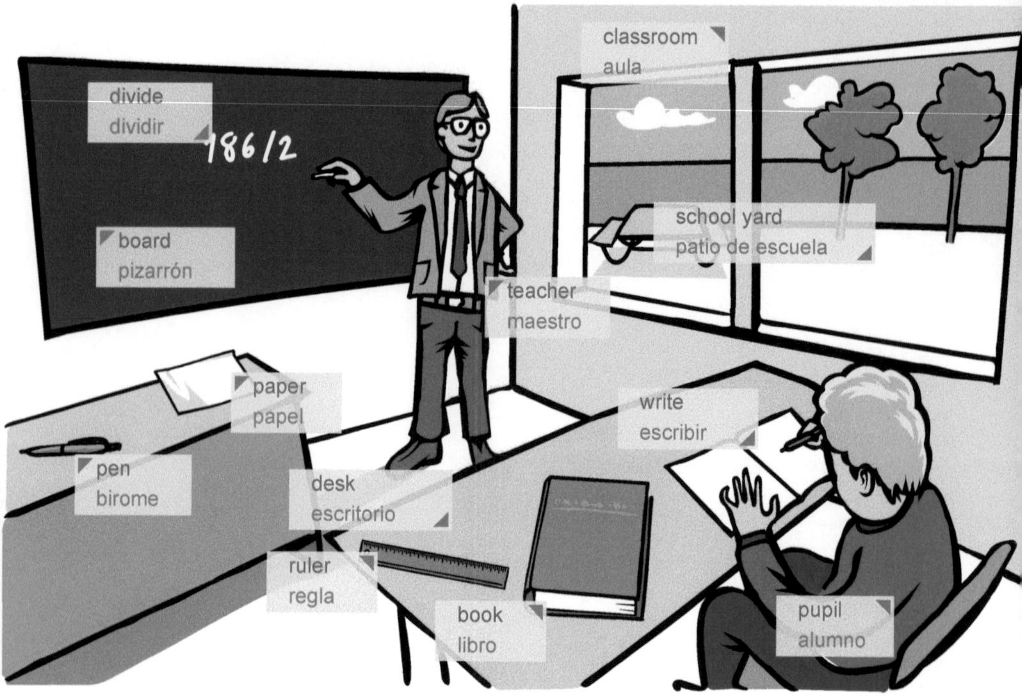
classroom
aula
divide
dividir
186/2
board
pizarrón
school yard
patio de escuela
teacher
maestro
paper
papel
write
escribir
pen
birome
desk
escritorio
ruler
regla
book
libro
pupil
alumno

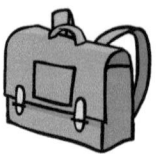

satchel

mochila

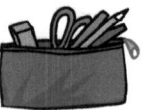

pencil case

caja de lápices

pencil

lápiz

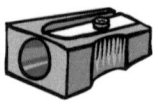

pencil sharpener

sacapuntas

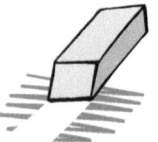

rubber

goma (de borrar)

drawing pad

bloc de dibujo

drawing

dibujo

paintbrush

pincel

paint box

caja de pinturas

scissors

tijera

glue

pegamento

exercise book

cuaderno de ejercicios

homework

tarea

number

número

2+2

add

sumar

5-2

subtract

restar

2×2

multiply

multiplicar

calculate

calcular

A

letter

letra

ABCDEFG
HIJKLMN
OPQRSTU
VWXYZ

alphabet

abecedario

word

palabra

text

texto

read

leer

chalk

tiza

lesson

lección

register

cuaderno de clase

examination

examen

certificate

certificado

school uniform

uniforme escolar

education

educación

encyclopedia

enciclopedia

university

universidad

microscope

microscopio

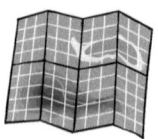

map

mapa

waste-paper basket

tacho (de basura)

travel
viaje

hotel
hotel
Grand
hostel
hostel
ROOMS
EXCHANGE
currency exchange office
casa de cambio
suitcase
valija
car
auto

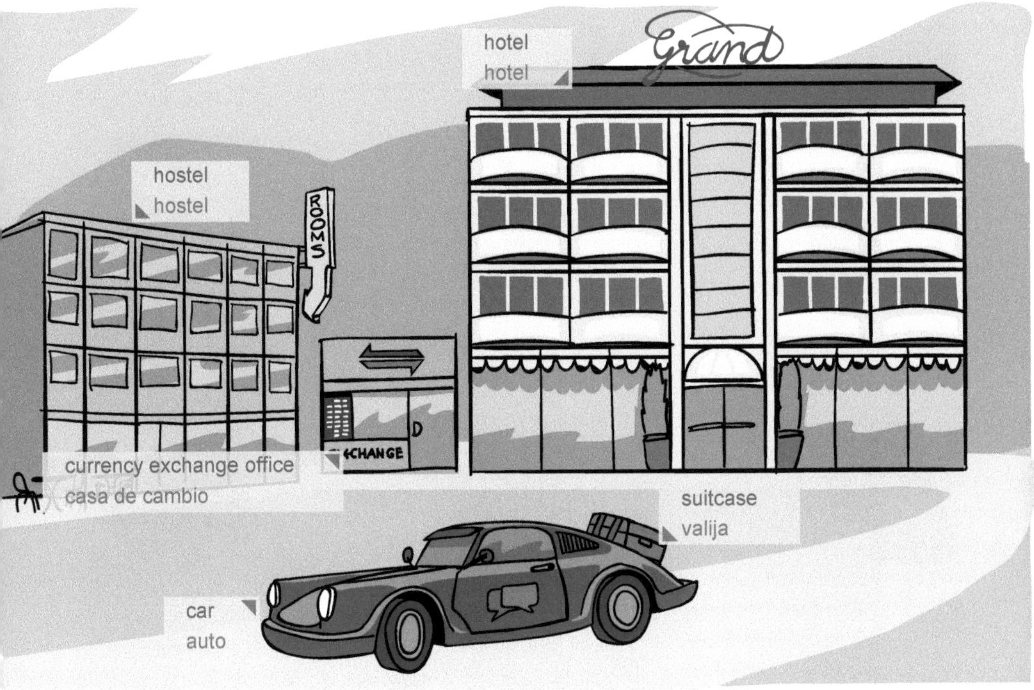

language
idioma

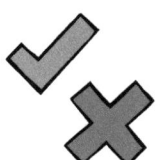

yes / no
sí / no

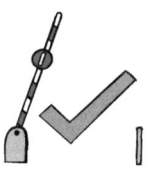

Okay
Está bien

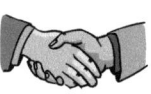

hello
hola

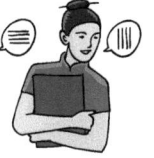

translator
traductor

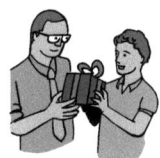

Thank you
Gracias

how much is…?

¿cuánto cuesta…?

I don´t get it

No entiendo

problem

problema

Good evening!

¡Buenas tardes!

Good morning!

¡Buenos días!

Good night!

¡Buenas noches!

goodbye

adiós

direction

dirección

luggage

equipaje

bag

bolso

backpack

mochila

guest

invitado

room

habitación

sleeping bag

bolsa de dormir

tent

carpa

tourist information	beach	credit card
información turística	playa	tarjeta de crédito

breakfast	lunch	dinner
desayuno	almuerzo	cena

Ticket	elevator	stamp
pasaje	ascensor	sello

border	customs	embassy
frontera	aduana	embajada

visa	passport	
visa	pasaporte	

transport
transporte

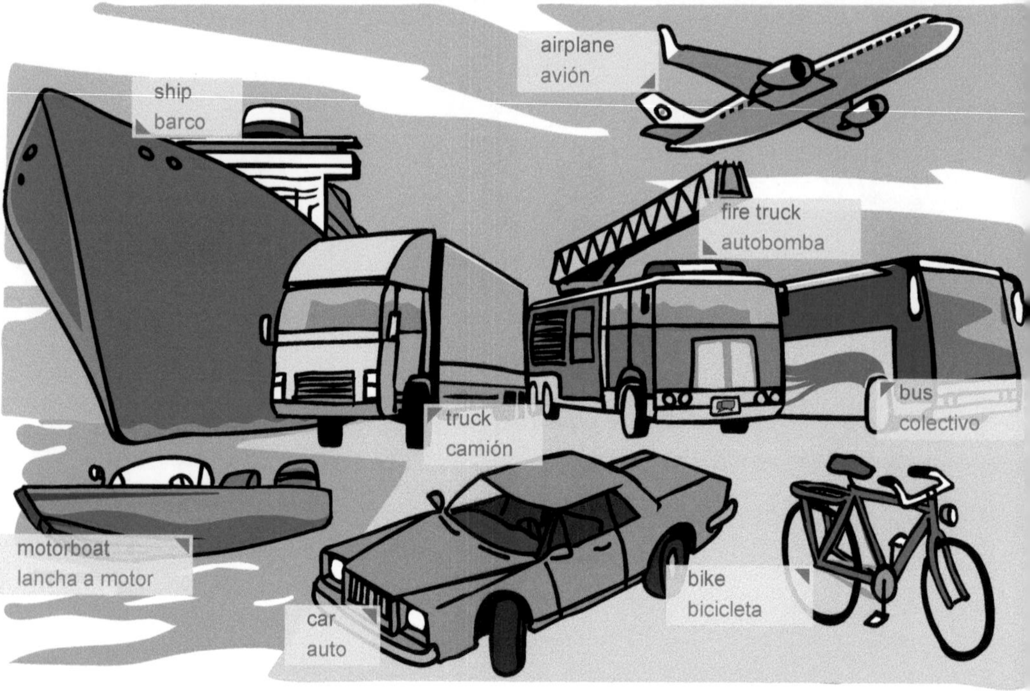

airplane
avión
ship
barco
fire truck
autobomba
bus
colectivo
truck
camión
motorboat
lancha a motor
bike
bicicleta
car
auto

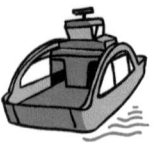

ferry

ferry

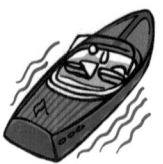

boat

bote

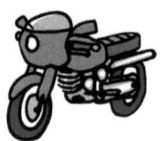

motorbike

moto

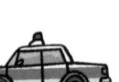

police car

patrullero

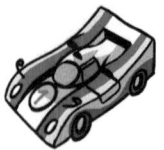

racing car

auto de carreras

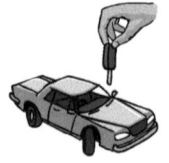

rental car

auto de alquiler

car sharing

alquiler de autos

tow truck

grúa

garbage truck

camión de basura

engine

motor

fuel

nafta

fuel station

estación de servicio

traffic sign

señal de tránsito

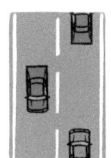

traffic

tránsito

traffic jam

embotellamiento

parking lot

estacionamiento

train station

estación de tren

tracks

vías

train

tren

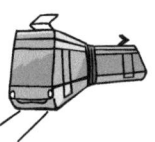

tram

tranvía

wagon

vagón

transport - transporte

helicopter

helicóptero

airport

aeropuerto

tower

torre

passenger

pasajero

container

contenedor

carton

caja de cartón

cart

carretilla

basket

canasta

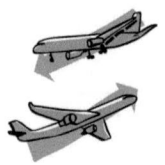

take off / land

despegar / aterrizar

city
ciudad

village

pueblo

city center

centro de ciudad

house

casa

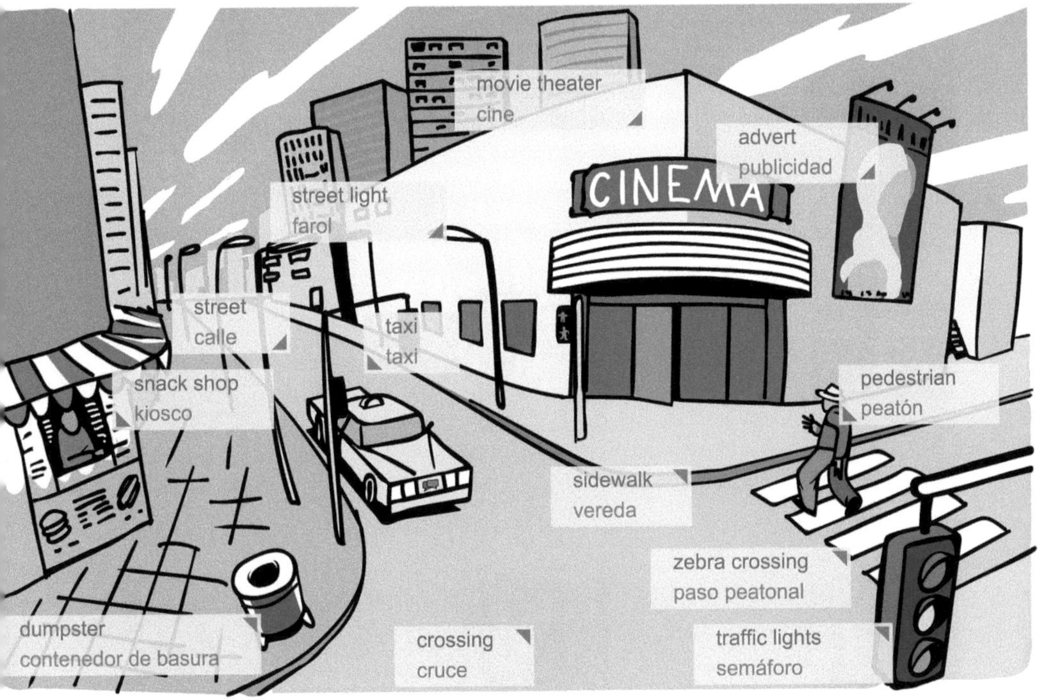

movie theater
cine
CINEMA
advert
publicidad
street light
farol
street
calle
taxi
taxi
snack shop
kiosco
pedestrian
peatón
sidewalk
vereda
zebra crossing
paso peatonal
dumpster
contenedor de basura
crossing
cruce
traffic lights
semáforo

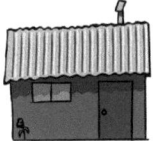

hut

cabaña

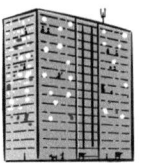

apartment

departamento

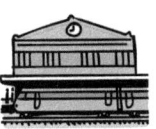

train station

estación de tren

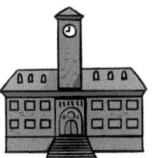

city hall

municipalidad

MUSEUM

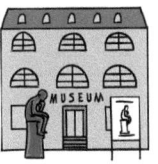

museum

museo

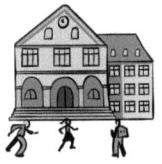

school

colegio

university

universidad

bank

banco

hospital

hospital

hotel

hotel

pharmacy

farmacia

office

oficina

book shop

librería

shop

negocio

flower shop

florería

supermarket

supermercado

market

mercado

department store

grandes tiendas

fishmonger's shop

pescadería

mall

centro comercial

harbor

puerto

park
parque

bench
banco

bridge
puente

stairs
escaleras

subway
subte

tunnel
túnel

bus stop
parada del colectivo

bar
bar

restaurant
restaurante

postbox
buzón

street sign
letrero

parking meter
parquímetro

zoo
zoológico

swimming pool
pileta

mosque
mezquita

farm

granja

pollution

contaminación

cemetery

cementerio

church

iglesia

playground

juegos infantiles

temple

templo

landscape

paisaje

leaf
hoja

signpost
poste indicador

path
camino

meadow
pradera

stone
piedra

hiker
excursionista

tree
árbol

river
río

grass
hierba

flower
flor

valley

valle

hill

montaña

lake

lago

forest

bosque

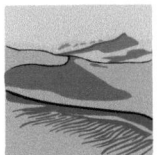

desert

desierto

volcano

volcán

castle

castillo

rainbow

arco iris

mushroom

champiñón

palm tree

palmera

mosquito

mosquito

fly

mosca

ant

hormiga

bee

abeja

spider

araña

landscape - paisaje

beetle

escarabajo

frog

rana

squirrel

ardilla

hedgehog

erizo

hare

liebre

owl

lechuza

bird

pájaro

swan

cisne

boar

jabalí

deer

ciervo

moose

alce

dam

presa

wind turbine

aerogenerador

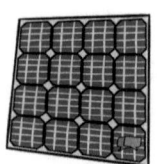

solar panel

panel solar

climate

clima

restaurant
restaurante

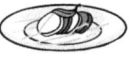

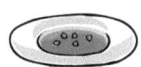

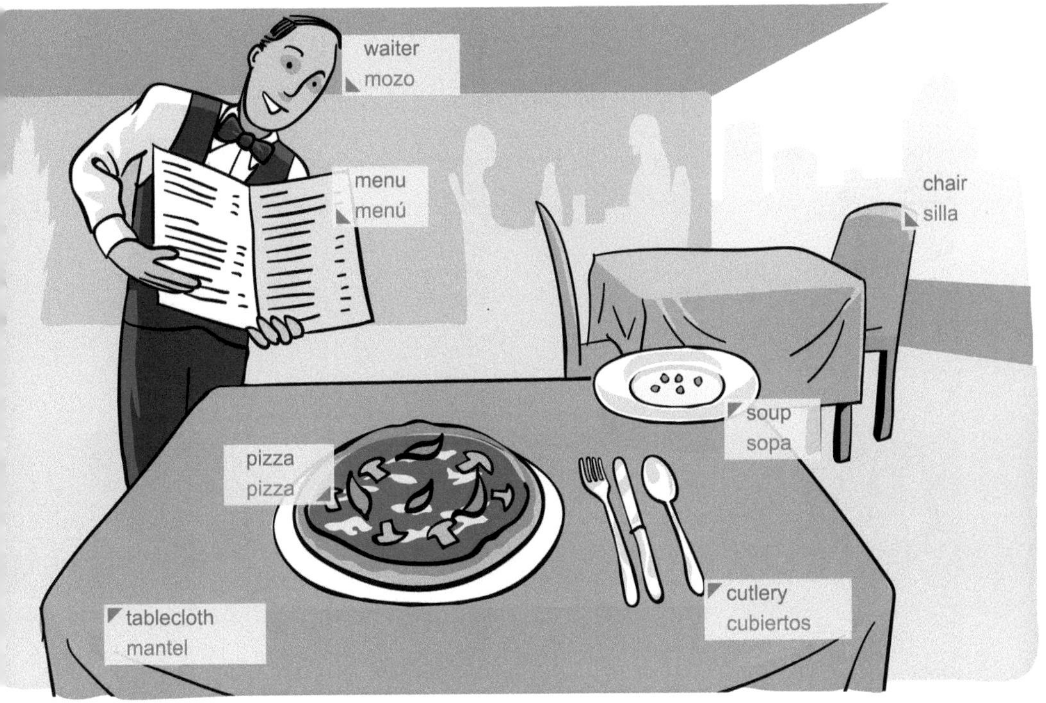
waiter
mozo
menu
menú
chair
silla
soup
sopa
pizza
pizza
tablecloth
mantel
cutlery
cubiertos

starter

entrada

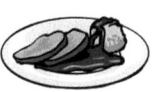

main course

plato principal

dessert

postre

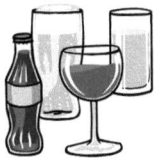

drinks

bebidas

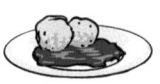

food

comida

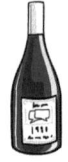

bottle

botella

fast food

comida rápida

street food

comida callejera

teapot

tetera

sugar bowl

azucarera

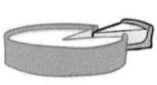

portion

porción

espresso machine

cafetera expreso

high chair

sillita alta

bill

cuenta

tray

bandeja

knife

cuchillo

fork

tenedor

spoon

cuchara

teaspoon

cucharita

serviette

servilleta

glass

vaso

restaurant - restaurante

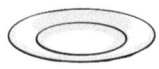

plate

plato

soup plate

plato hondo

saucer

plato

sauce

salsa

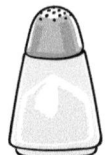

salt shaker

salero

pepper mill

molinillo de pimienta

vinegar

vinagre

oil

aceite

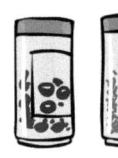

spices

especias

ketchup

kétchup

mustard

mostaza

mayonnaise

mayonesa

supermarket
supermercado

special offer
oferta especial
FOR
customer
cliente
dairy products
lácteos
fruit
fruta
shopping cart
changuito

BUTCHERS

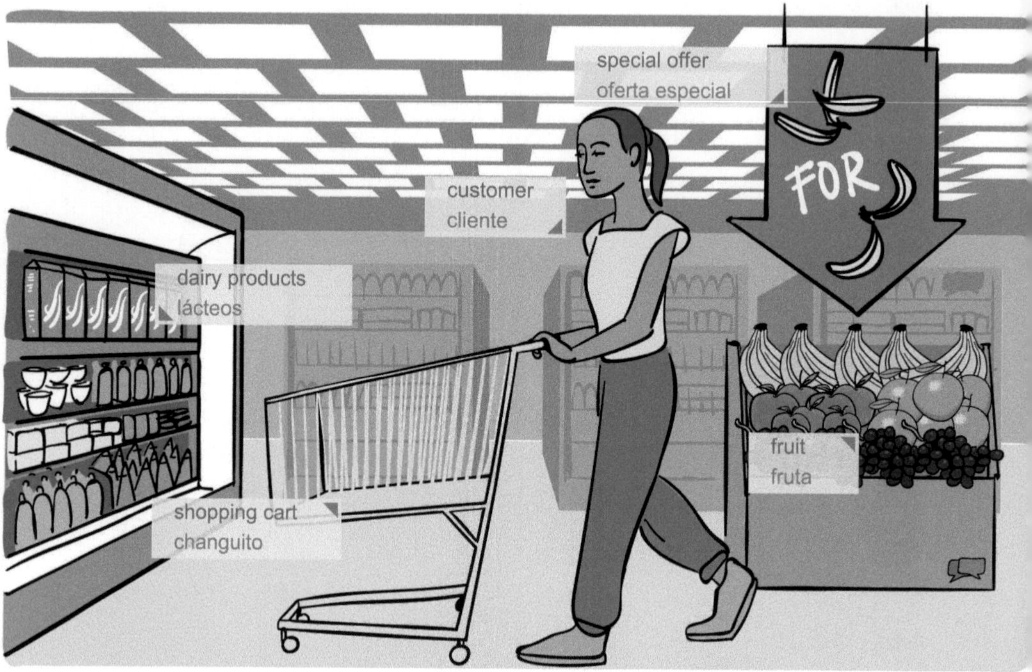

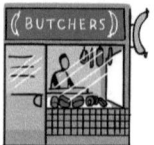

butcher's shop

carnicería

BAKERY

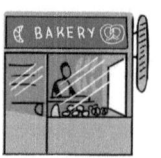

bakery

panadería

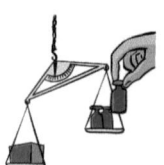

weigh

pesar

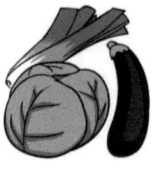

vegetables

verduras

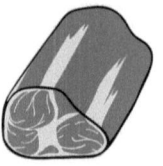

meat

carne

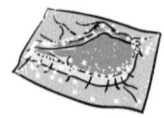

frozen food

alimentos congelados

cold cuts

fiambres

canned food

alimentos enlatados

detergent

detergente en polvo

candy

golosinas

household products

electrodomésticos

cleaning products

productos de limpieza

sales representative

vendedora

cash register

caja

cashier

cajero

shopping list

lista de compras

opening hours

horario de atención

wallet

billetera

credit card

tarjeta de crédito

bag

cartera

plastic bag

bolsa de plástico

drinks
bebidas

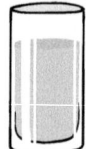

water
....
agua

juice
....
jugo

milk
....
leche

coke
....
bebida cola

wine
....
vino

beer
....
cerveza

alcohol
....
alcohol

cocoa
....
cacao

tea
....
té

coffee
....
café

espresso
....
café expreso

cappuccino
....
cappuccino

banana

banana

apple

manzana

orange

naranja

melon

melón

lemon

limón

carrot

zanahoria

garlic

ajo

bamboo

bambú

onion

cebolla

mushroom

champiñón

nuts

nueces

noodles

fideos

spaghetti

tallarines

rice

arroz

salad

ensalada

fries

papas fritas

fried potatoes

papas fritas

pizza

pizza

hamburger

hamburguesa

sandwich

sándwich

escalope

churrasco

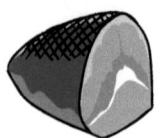

ham

jamón

salami

salame

sausage

salchicha

chicken

pollo

roast

asado

fish

pescado

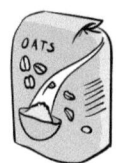

porridge oats

copos de avena

muesli

muesli

cornflakes

copos de maíz

flour

harina

croissant

medialuna

bread roll

pancito

bread

pan

toast

tostada

cookies

galletitas

butter

manteca

curd

cuajada

cake

torta

egg

huevo

fried egg

huevo frito

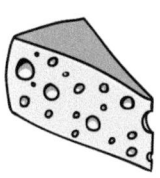

cheese

queso

ice cream

helado

sugar

azúcar

honey

miel

jelly

mermelada

nougat cream

pasta de chocolate

curry

curry

farm
granja

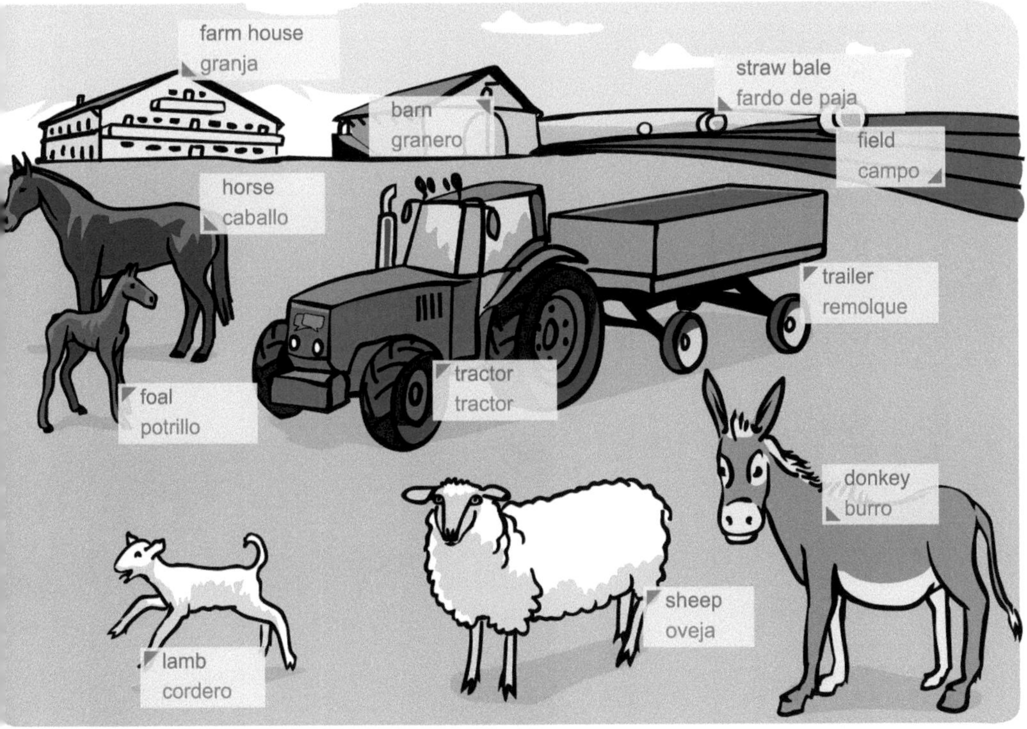
farm house
granja
barn
granero
straw bale
fardo de paja
field
campo
horse
caballo
trailer
remolque
tractor
tractor
foal
potrillo
donkey
burro
sheep
oveja
lamb
cordero

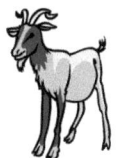

goat

cabra

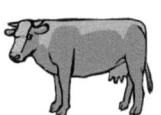

cow

vaca

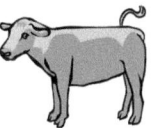

calf

ternero

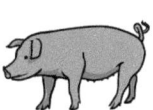

pig

cerdo

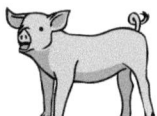

piglet

lechón

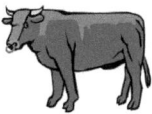

bull

toro

goose

ganso

duck

pato

chick

pollo

hen

gallina

cockerel

gallo

rat

rata

cat

gato

mouse

ratón

ox

buey

dog

perro

dog house

cucha

garden hose

manguera

watering can

regadera

scythe

guadaña

plow

arado

sickle

hoz

hoe

azada

pitchfork

horquilla

axe

hacha

pushcart

carretilla

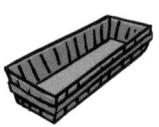

trough

abrevadero

milk can

lechera

sack

bolsa

fence

reja

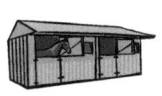

stable

establo

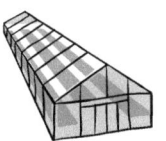

greenhouse

invernadero

soil

suelo

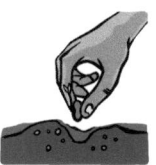

seed

semilla

fertilizer

fertilizador

combine harvester

cosechadora

harvest

cosechar

harvest

cosecha

yams

batatas

wheat

trigo

soya

soja

potato

papa

corn

maíz

rapeseed

semilla de colza

fruit tree

árbol frutal

manioc

mandioca

grain

cereales

house

casa

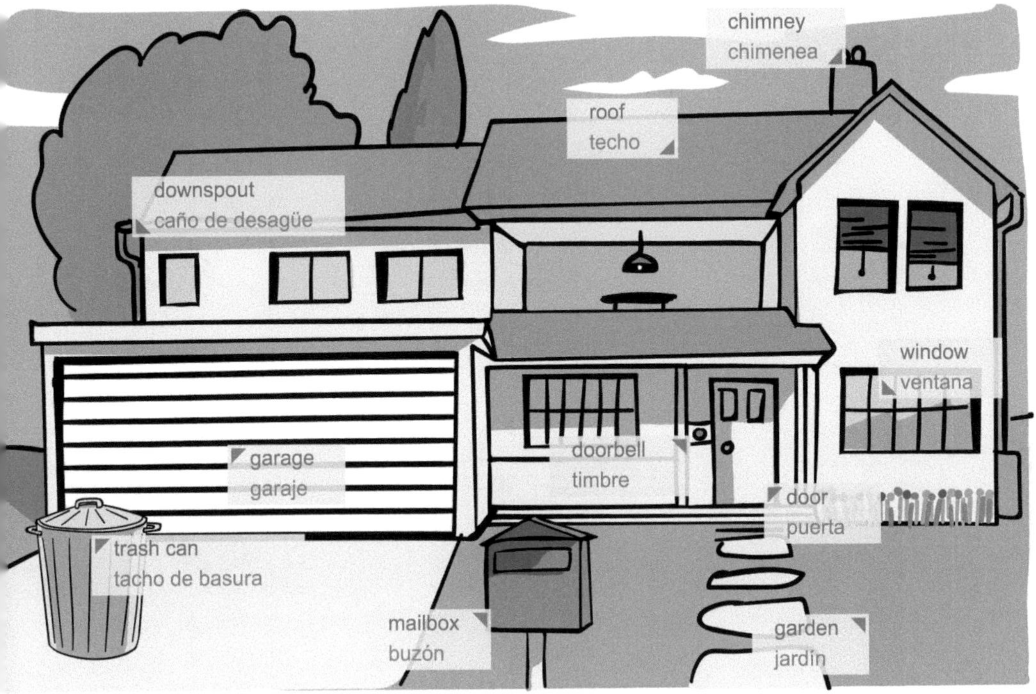
chimney
chimenea
roof
techo
downspout
caño de desagüe
window
ventana
doorbell
timbre
garage
garaje
door
puerta
trash can
tacho de basura
mailbox
buzón
garden
jardín

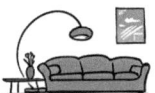

living room

living

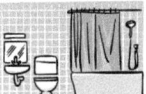

bathroom

baño

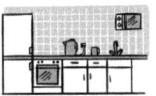

kitchen

cocina

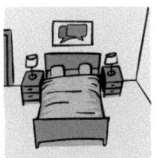

bedroom

dormitorio

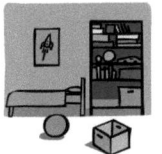

kids room

cuarto de los chicos

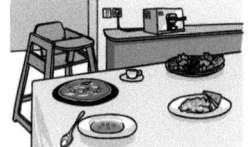

dining room

comedor

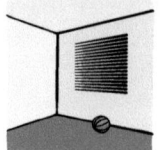

floor

piso

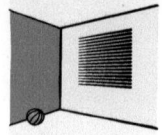

wall

pared

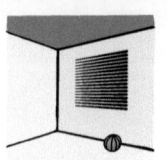

ceiling

cielorraso

cellar

sótano

sauna

sauna

balcony

balcón

terrace

terraza

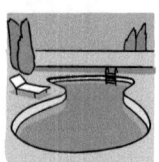

pool

pileta

lawn mower

cortadora de pasto

sheet

sábana

bedspread

acolchado

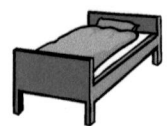

bed

cama

broom

escoba

bucket

balde

switch

interruptor

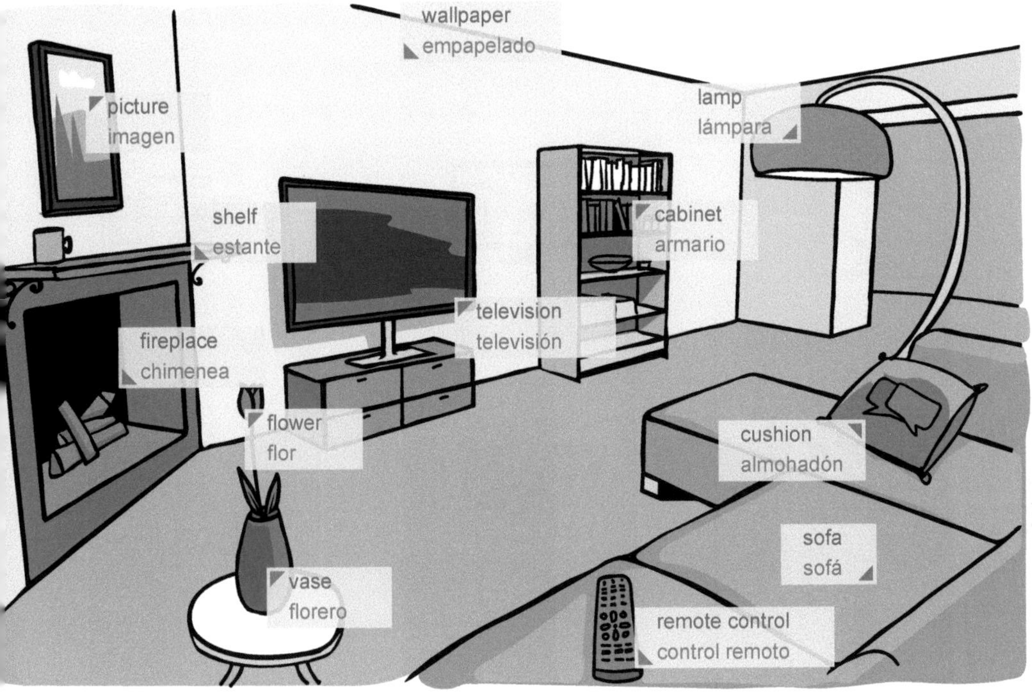

wallpaper
empapelado

picture
imagen

lamp
lámpara

shelf
estante

cabinet
armario

fireplace
chimenea

television
televisión

flower
flor

cushion
almohadón

vase
florero

sofa
sofá

remote control
control remoto

carpet
alfombra

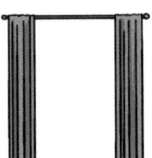

drape
cortina

table
mesa

chair
silla

rocking chair
mecedora

armchair
sillón

book

libro

blanket

frazada

decoration

decoración

firewood

leña

film

película

stereo system

equipo de música

key

llave

newspaper

diario

painting

pintura

poster

póster

radio

radio

notebook

cuaderno

vacuum cleaner

aspiradora

cactus

cactus

candle

vela

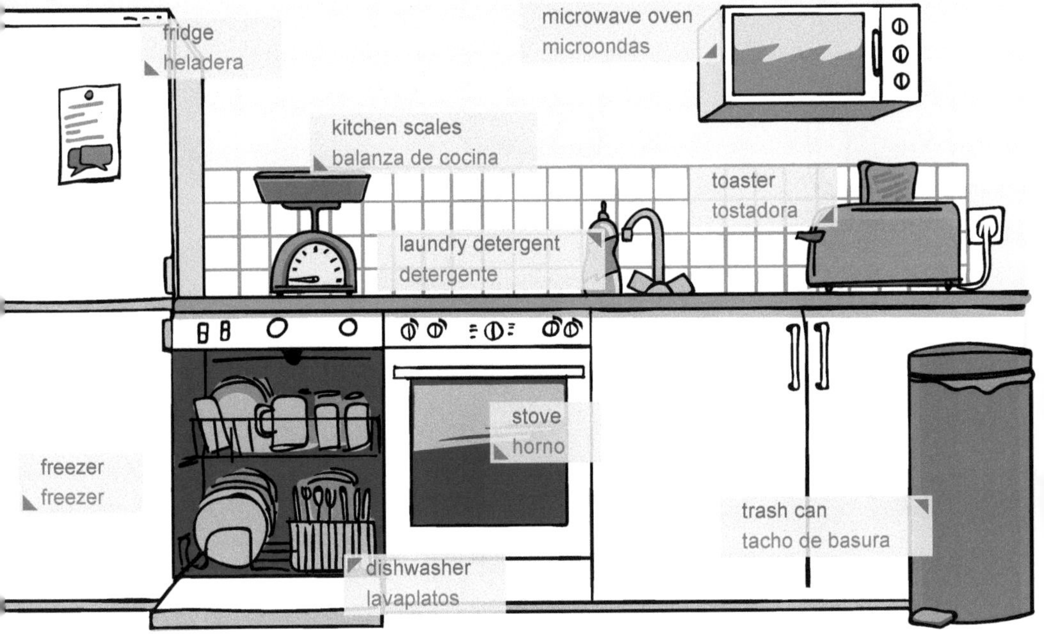

fridge
heladera

microwave oven
microondas

kitchen scales
balanza de cocina

toaster
tostadora

laundry detergent
detergente

stove
horno

freezer
freezer

trash can
tacho de basura

dishwasher
lavaplatos

cooker	pot	cast-iron pot
cocina	olla	olla de hierro fundido
wok / kadai	pan	kettle
wok	sartén	pava

steamer

vaporera

baking tray

bandeja de horno

crockery

vajilla

mug

taza

bowl

bol

chopsticks

palitos

ladle

cucharón

spatula

estpátula

whisk

batidora

strainer

colador

sieve

colador

grater

rallador

mortar

mortero

barbecue

parrilla

fireplace

fogata

chopping board

tabla de picar

rolling pin

palo de amasar

corkscrew

sacacorchos

can

lata

can opener

abrelatas

oven cloth

manopla

sink

pileta

brush

cepillo

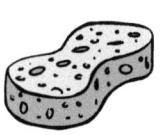

sponge

esponja

blender

batidora

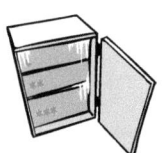

deep freezer

congelador

baby bottle

mamadera

tap

canilla

bathroom

baño

heating
calefacción
shower
ducha
towel
toalla
shower curtain
cortina de ducha
bubble bath
baño de espuma
bathtub
bañadera
glass
vaso
washing machine
lavarropas
tap
canilla
tiles
baldosas
potty
pelela
sink
pileta

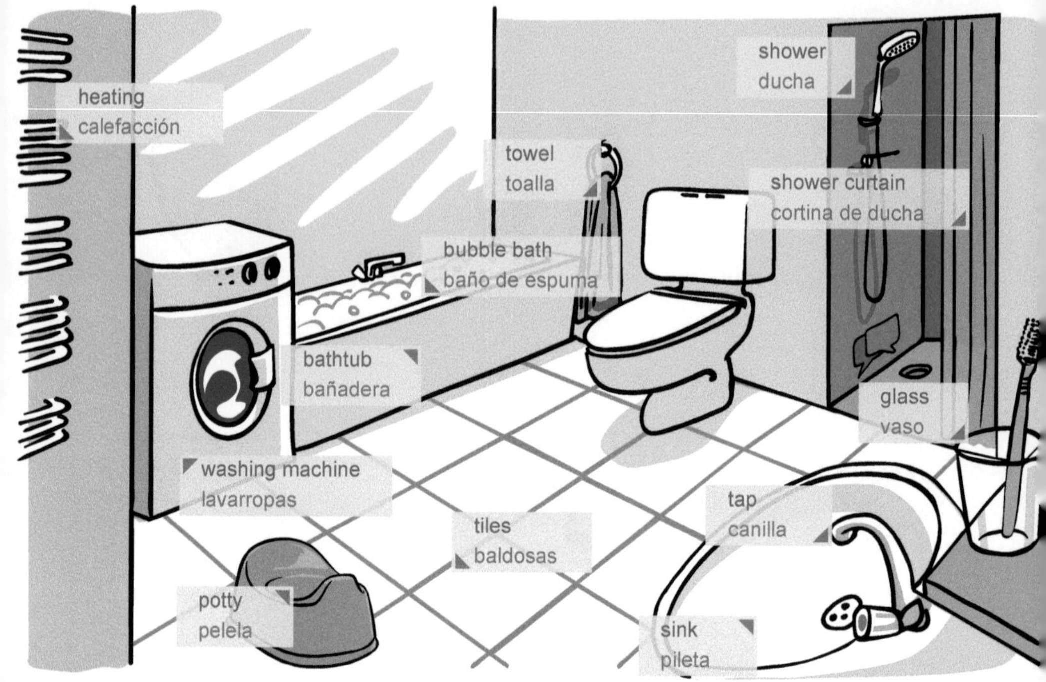

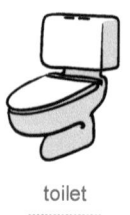

toilet

inodoro

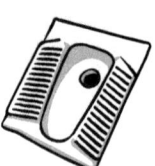

squat toilet

letrina

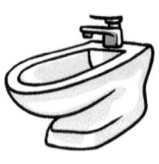

bidet

bidé

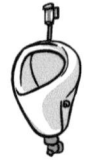

urinal

mingitorio

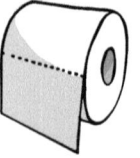

toilet paper

papel higiénico

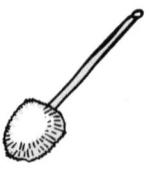

toilet brush

cepillo para el inodoro

toothbrush

cepillo de dientes

toothpaste

dentífrico

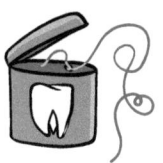

dental floss

hilo dental

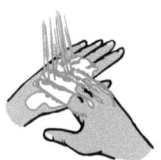

wash

lavar

hand shower

ducha de mano

douche

ducha higiénica

basin

palangana

back brush

cepillo para espalda

soap

jabón

shower gel

gel de ducha

shampoo

shampoo

flannel

toallita

drain

desagüe

creme

crema

deodorant

desodorante

mirror

espejo

hand mirror

espejito

razor

maquinita de afeitar

shaving foam

espuma de afeitar

aftershave

aftershave

comb

peine

brush

cepillo

hair-dryer

secador de pelo

hairspray

spray

makeup

maquillaje

lipstick

lápiz de labios

nail varnish

esmalte para uñas

cotton wool

algodón

nail scissors

tijera para uñas

perfume

perfume

washbag

portacosméticos

stool

banqueta

weighing scales

balanza

bathrobe

bata

rubber gloves

guantes de goma

tampon

tampón

sanitary towel

toallita femenina

chemical toilet

baño químico

kids room
cuarto de los chicos

alarm clock
despertador
cuddly toy
peluche
toy car
coche de juguete
rattle
sonajero
doll's house
casa de muñecas
present
regalo

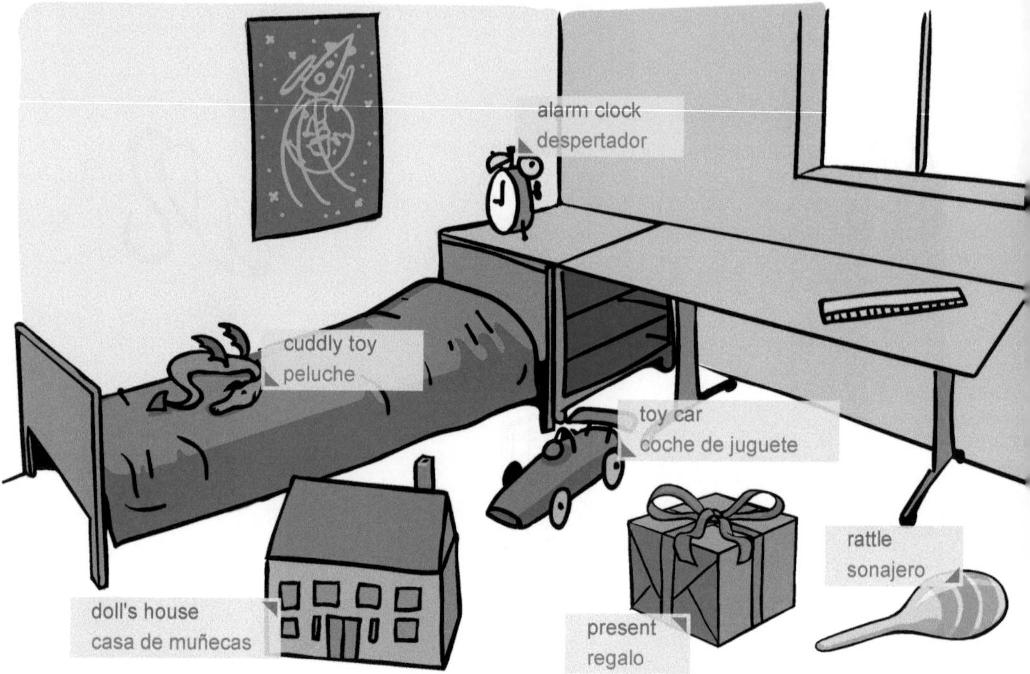

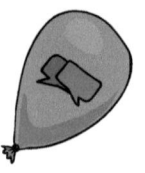

balloon

globo

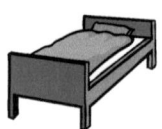

bed

cama

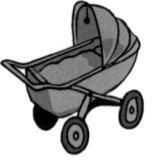

stroller

cochecito

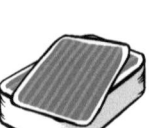

deck of cards

cartas

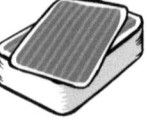

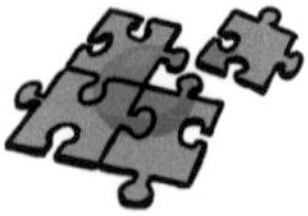

jigsaw

rompecabezas

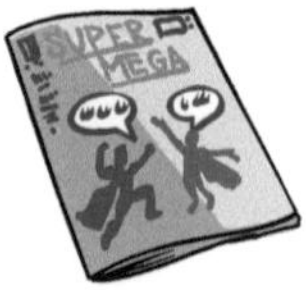

comic

historieta

lego bricks

piezas de lego

toy blocks

ladrillos de juguete

action figure

figura de acción

romper suit

enterito (de bebé)

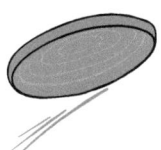

frisbee

frisbee

mobile

móvil para bebés

board game

juego de mesa

dice

dados

model train set

tren eléctrico

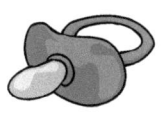

pacifier

chupete

party

fiesta

picture book

libro de cuentos ilustrado

ball

pelota

doll

muñeca

play

jugar

sandpit

arenero

swing

hamaca

toys

juguetes

video game console

consola de videojuegos

tricycle

triciclo

teddy bear

osito de peluche

wardrobe

armario

clothing

ropa

socks

medias

stockings

medias panty

tights

calzas

scarf
bufanda

belt
cinturón

umbrella
paraguas

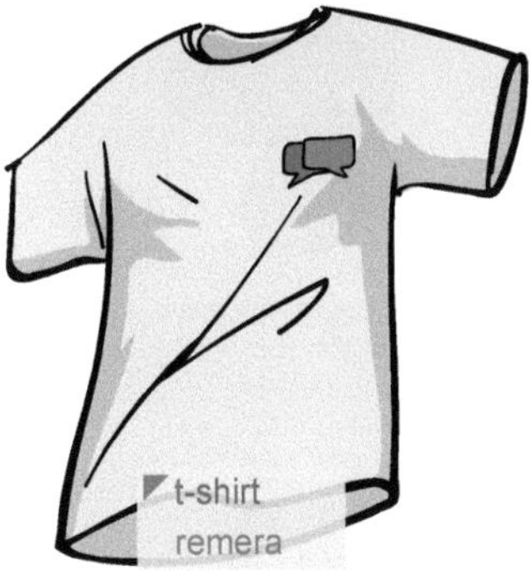

t-shirt
remera

sneakers
zapatillas

boots
botas

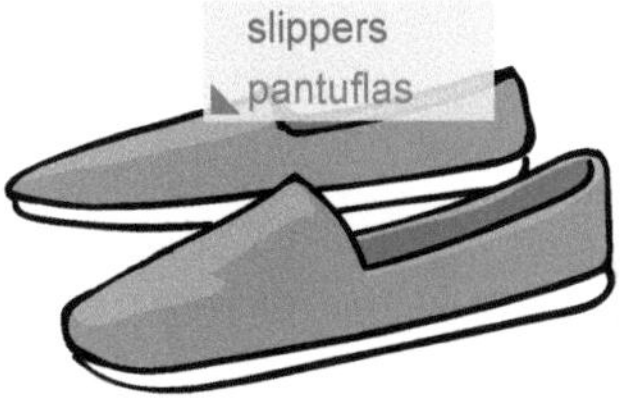

slippers
pantuflas

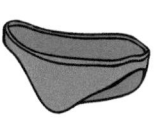

sandals
sandalias

shoes
zapatos

rubber boots
botas de goma

underwear
ropa interior

bra
corpiño

undershirt
chaleco

clothing - ropa

body

body

pants

pantalones

jeans

jeans

skirt

pollera

blouse

blusa

shirt

camisa

pullover

pulóver

sweater

buzo

blazer

blazer

jacket

campera

coat

tapado

raincoat

piloto

costume

traje

dress

vestido

wedding dress

vestido de novia

suit

traje

nightgown

camisón

pajamas

pijama

sari

sari

headscarf

pañuelo para cabeza

turban

turbante

burka

burka

kaftan

caftán

abaya

abaya

swimsuit

traje de baño

trunks

short de baño

shorts

shorts

tracksuit

jogging

apron

delantal

gloves

guantes

button

botón

glasses

anteojos

bracelet

pulsera

necklace

collar

ring

anillo

earring

aro

cap

gorra

coat hanger

percha

hat

sombrero

tie

corbata

zip

cierre

helmet

casco

braces

tiradores

school uniform

uniforme escolar

uniform

uniforme

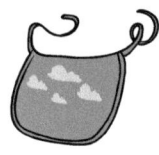

bib

babero

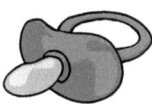

pacifier

chupete

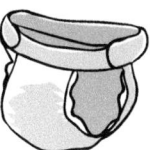

diaper

pañal

office
oficina

server
servidor
filing cabinet
archivero
paper
papel
printer
impresora
monitor
monitor
mouse
mouse
desk
escritorio
folder
carpeta
keyboard
teclado
waste-paper basket
tacho (de basura)
chair
silla
computer
computadora

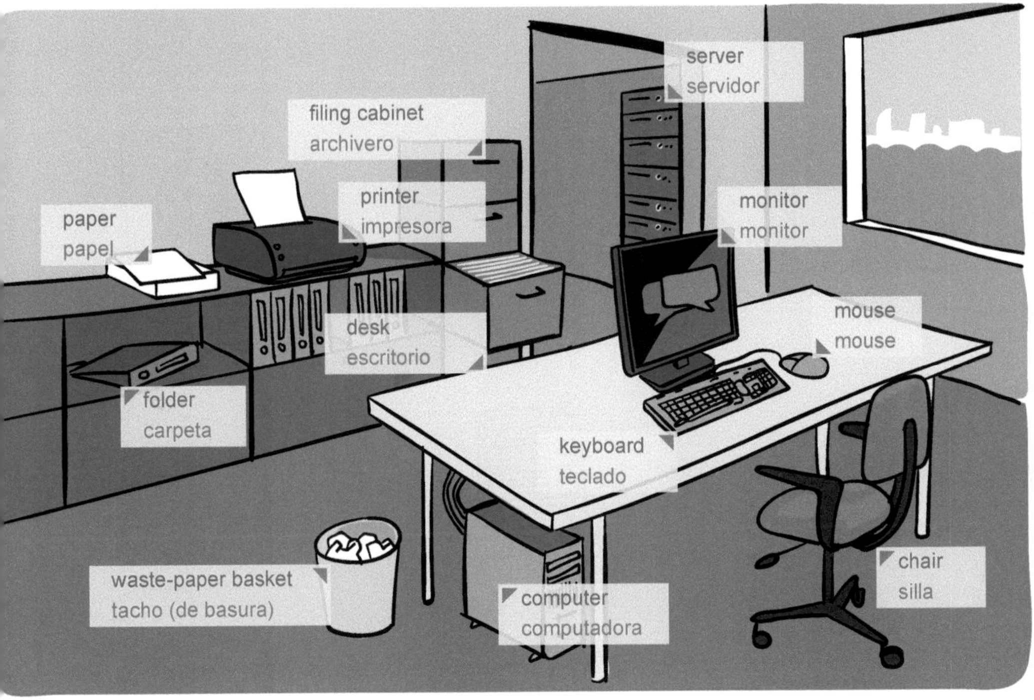

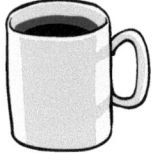

coffee mug

taza de café

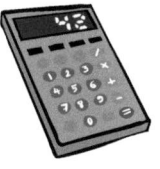

calculator

calculadora

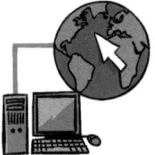

internet

internet

laptop

laptop

letter

carta

message

mensaje

cell phone

celular

network

red

photocopier

fotocopiadora

software

software

telephone

teléfono

plug socket

tomacorriente

fax machine

fax

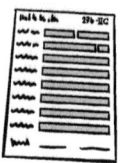

form

formulario

document

documento

buy

comprar

pay

pagar

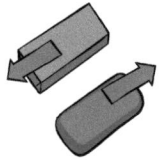

trade

hacer negocios

money

dinero

 **USD**

dollar

dólar

 **EUR**

euro

euro

 **JPY**

yen

yen

 **RUB**

rouble

rublo

 **CHF**

Swiss franc

franco suizo

 **CNY**

renminbi yuan

yuan

 **INR**

rupee

rupia

cash point

cajero automático

currency exchange office

casa de cambio

gold

oro

silver

plata

oil

petróleo

energy

energía

price

precio

contract

contrato

tax

impuesto

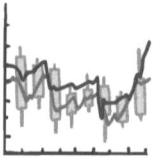

stock

acción

work

trabajar

employee

empleado

employer

empleador

factory

fábrica

shop

negocio

occupations
ocupaciones

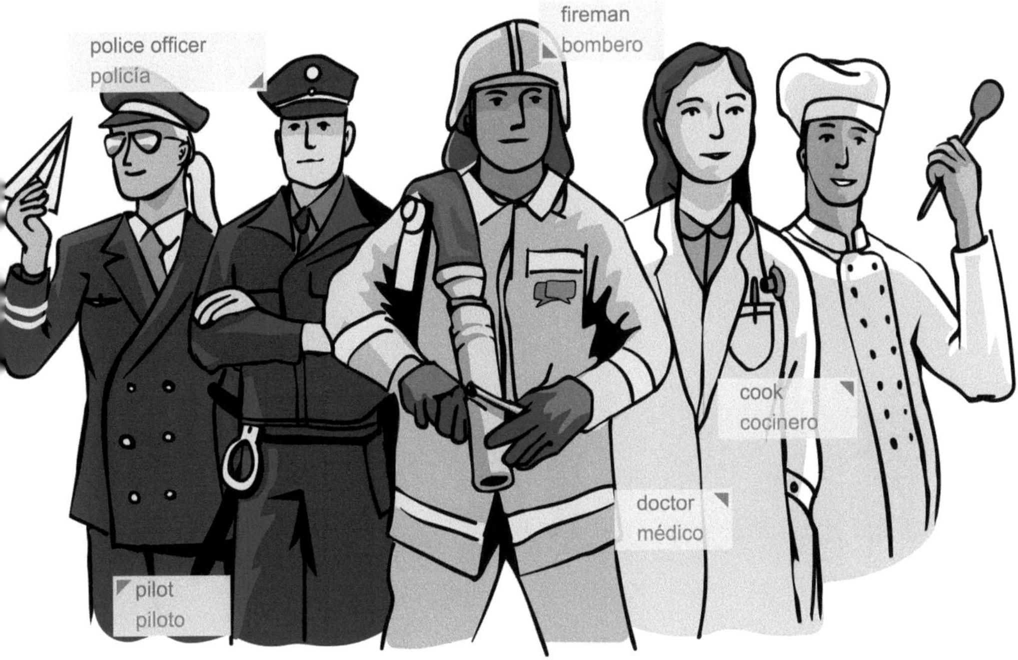
police officer
policía
fireman
bombero
cook
cocinero
doctor
médico
pilot
piloto

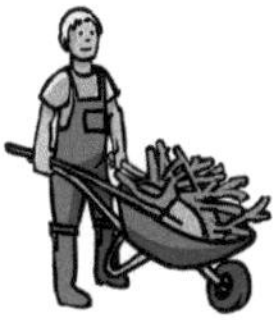

gardener

jardinero

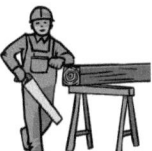

carpenter

carpintero

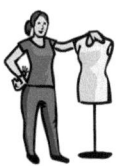

seamstress

modista

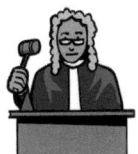

judge

juez

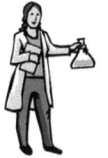

chemist

farmacéutico

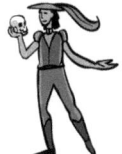

actor

actor

bus driver

colectivero

taxi driver

taxista

fisherman

pescador

cleaning lady

mucama

roofer

techista

waiter

mozo

hunter

cazador

painter

pintor

baker

panadero

electrician

electricista

builder

albañil

engineer

ingeniero

butcher

carnicero

plumber

plomero

postman

cartero

soldier

soldado

architect

arquitecto

cashier

cajero

florist

florista

hairdresser

peluquero

conductor

cobrador

mechanic

mecánico

captain

capitán

dentist

dentista

scientist

científico

rabbi

rabino

imam

imán

monk

monje

pastor

sacerdote

tools

herramientas

hammer
martillo
pliers
tenaza
screwdriver
destornillador
wrench
llave
torch
linterna

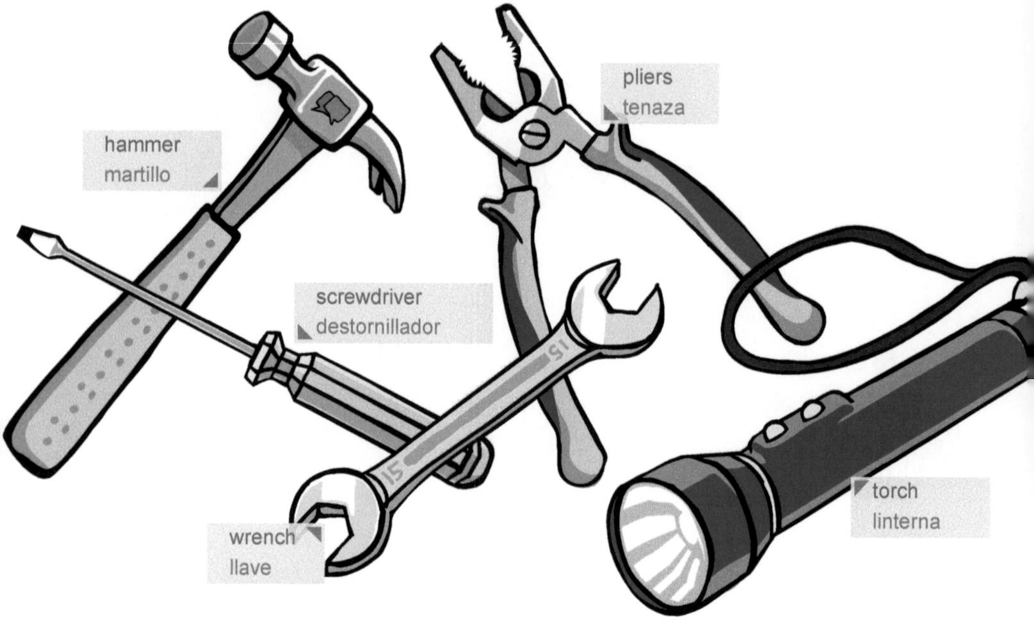

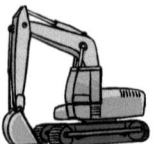

excavator

excavadora

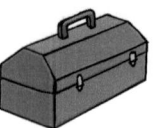

toolbox

caja de herramientas

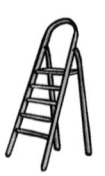

ladder

escalera portátil

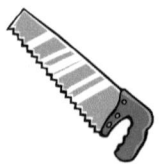

saw

sierra

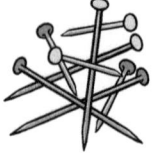

nails

clavos

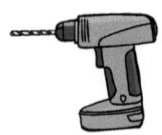

drill

taladro

repair
arreglar

shovel
pala de jardín

Damn!
¡Qué bronca!

dustpan
pala de plástico

paint can
tacho de pintura

screws
tornillos

musical instruments
instrumentos musicales

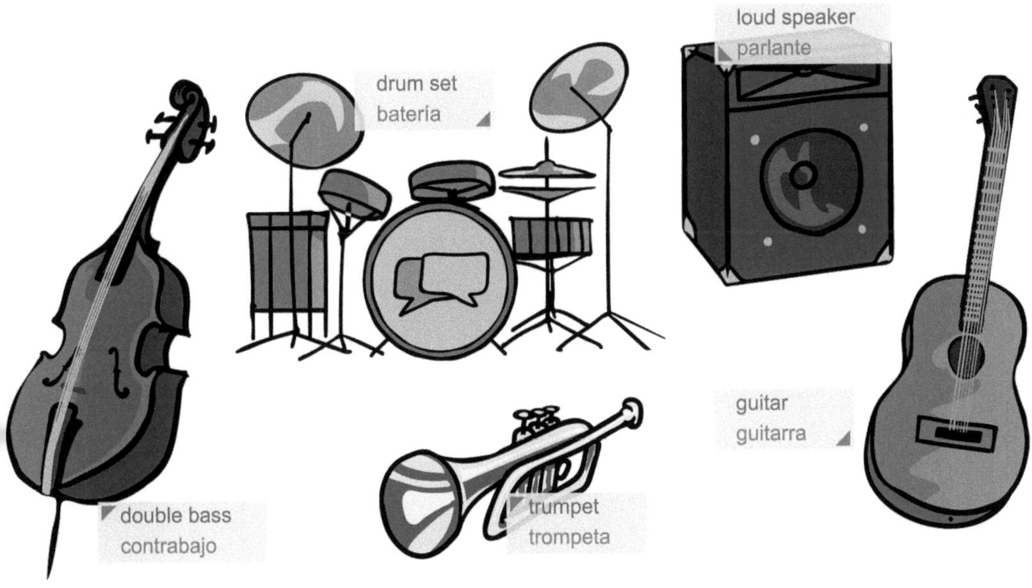

drum set
batería

loud speaker
parlante

double bass
contrabajo

trumpet
trompeta

guitar
guitarra

piano

piano

violin

violín

bass

bajo

timpani

timbales

drums

tambor

keyboard

teclado

saxophone

saxofón

flute

flauta

microphone

micrófono

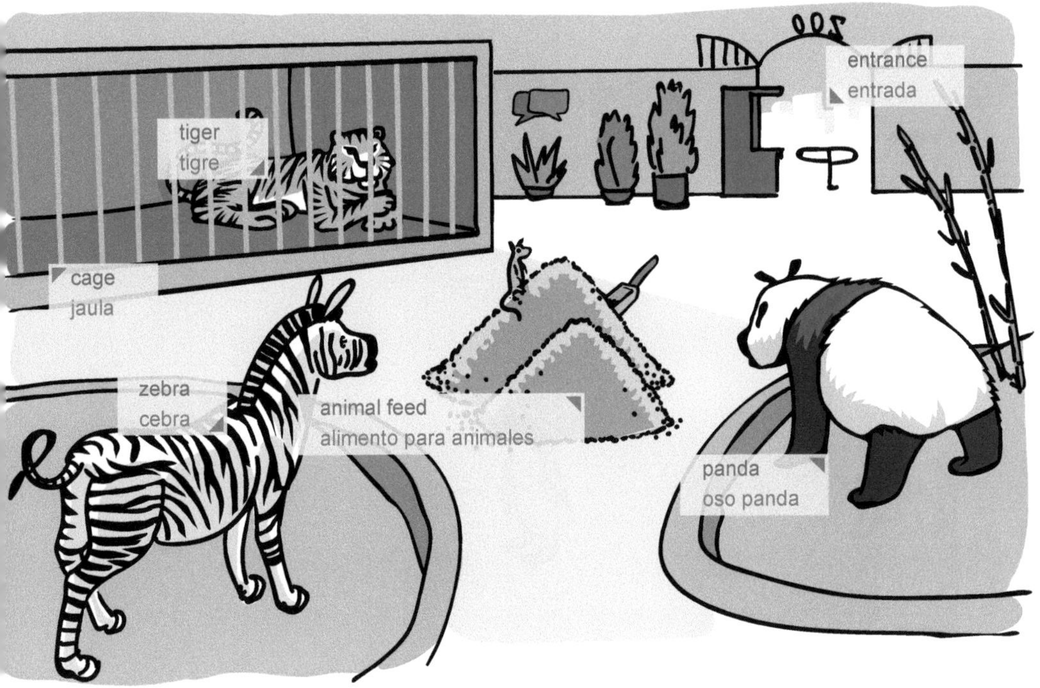

entrance
entrada

tiger
tigre

cage
jaula

zebra
cebra

animal feed
alimento para animales

panda
oso panda

animals

animales

elephant

elefante

kangaroo

canguro

rhino

rinoceronte

gorilla

gorila

bear

oso

camel

camello

ostrich

avestruz

lion

león

monkey

mono

flamingo

flamenco

parrot

loro

polar bear

oso polar

penguin

pingüino

shark

tiburón

peacock

pavo real

snake

serpiente

crocodile

cocodrilo

zookeeper

cuidador del zoológico

seal

foca

jaguar

jaguar

pony

poni

leopard

leopardo

hippo

hipopótamo

giraffe

jirafa

eagle

águila

boar

jabalí

fish

pescado

turtle

tortuga

walrus

morsa

fox

zorro

gazelle

gacela

sports

deportes

American football
fútbol americano

cycling
ciclismo

tennis
tenis

basketball
básquet

swimming
natación

boxing
boxeo

ice hockey
hockey sobre hielo

soccer

fútbol

badminton

bádminton

athletics

atletismo

handball

handball

skiing

esquí

polo

polo

jump
saltar

laugh
reír

hug
abrazar

walk
caminar

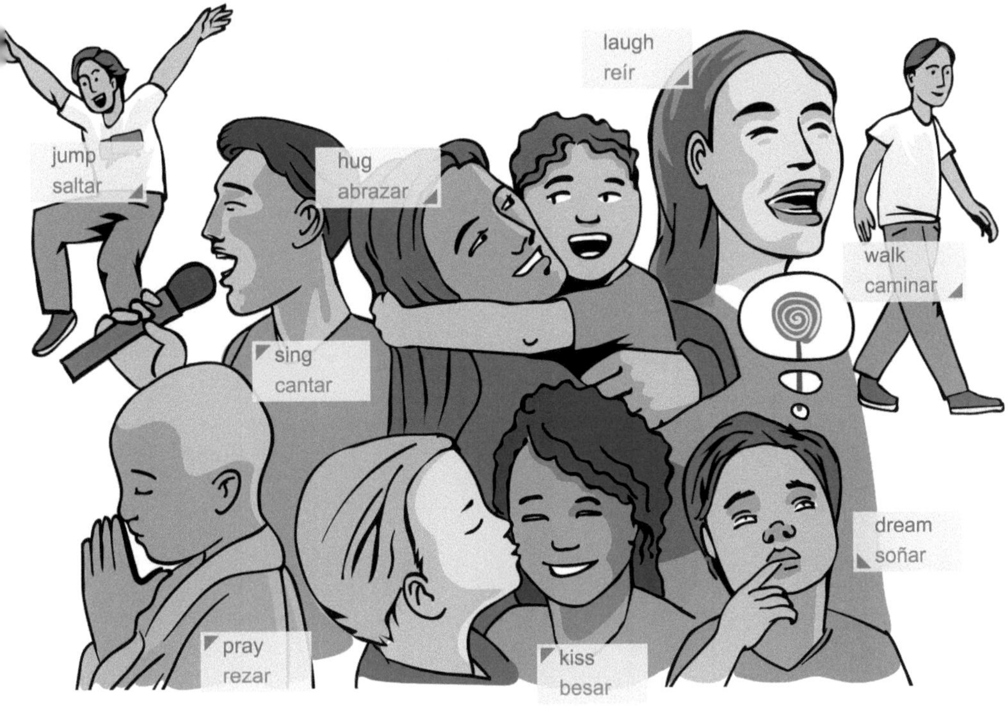

sing
cantar

dream
soñar

pray
rezar

kiss
besar

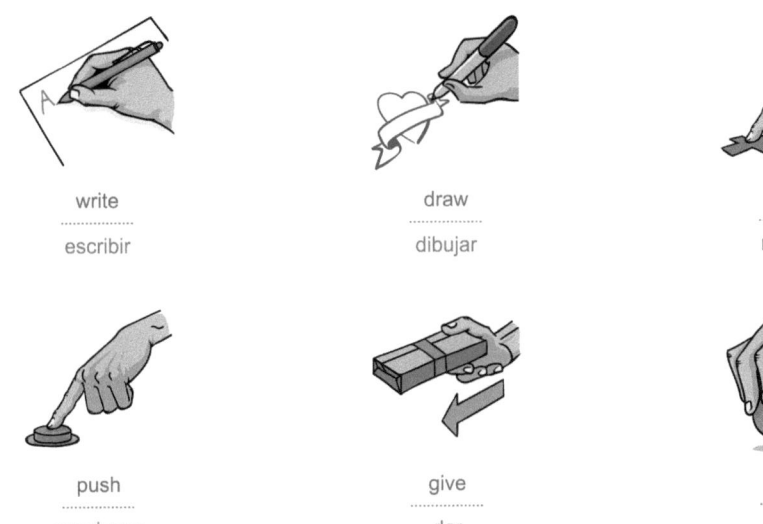

write	draw	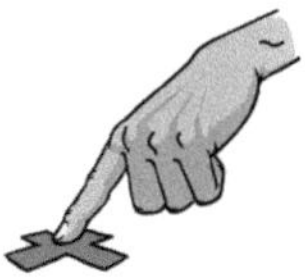 show
escribir	dibujar	mostrar
push	give	take
presionar	dar	tomar

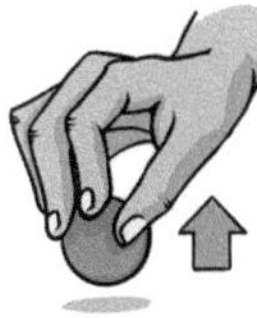

have

tener

do

hacer

be

ser

stand

estar parado

run

correr

pull

tirar

throw

tirar

fall

caer

lie

estar acostado

wait

esperar

carry

llevar

sit

estar sentado

get dressed

vestirse

sleep

dormir

wake up

despertar

look at

mirar

cry

llorar

stroke

acariciar

comb

peinar

talk

hablar

understand

entender

ask

preguntar

listen

escuchar

drink

beber

eat

comer

tidy up

ordenar

love

amar

cook

cocinar

drive

manejar

fly

volar

sail

navegar

calculate

calcular

read

leer

learn

aprender

work

trabajar

marry

casarse

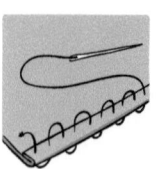

sew

coser

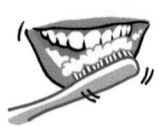

brush teeth

cepillarse los dientes

kill

matar

smoke

fumar

send

enviar

family
familia

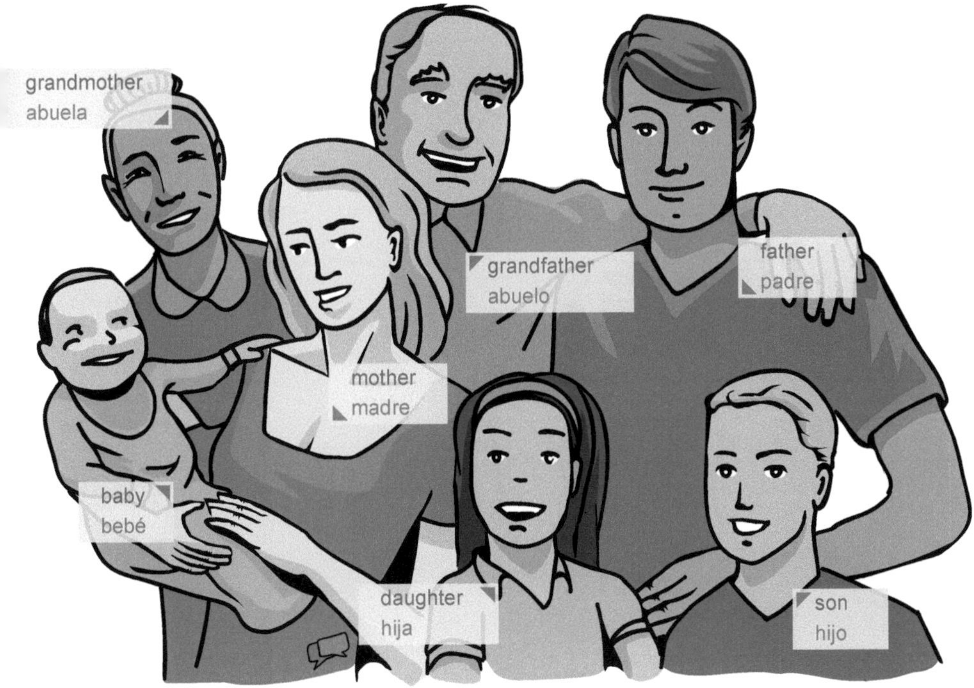
grandmother
abuela
grandfather
abuelo
father
padre
mother
madre
baby
bebé
daughter
hija
son
hijo

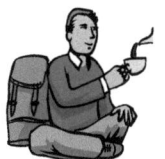

guest

invitado

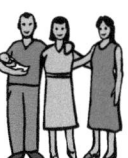

aunt

tía

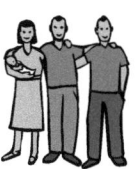

uncle

tío

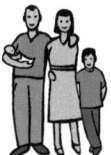

brother

hermano

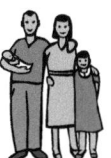

sister

hermana

body

cuerpo

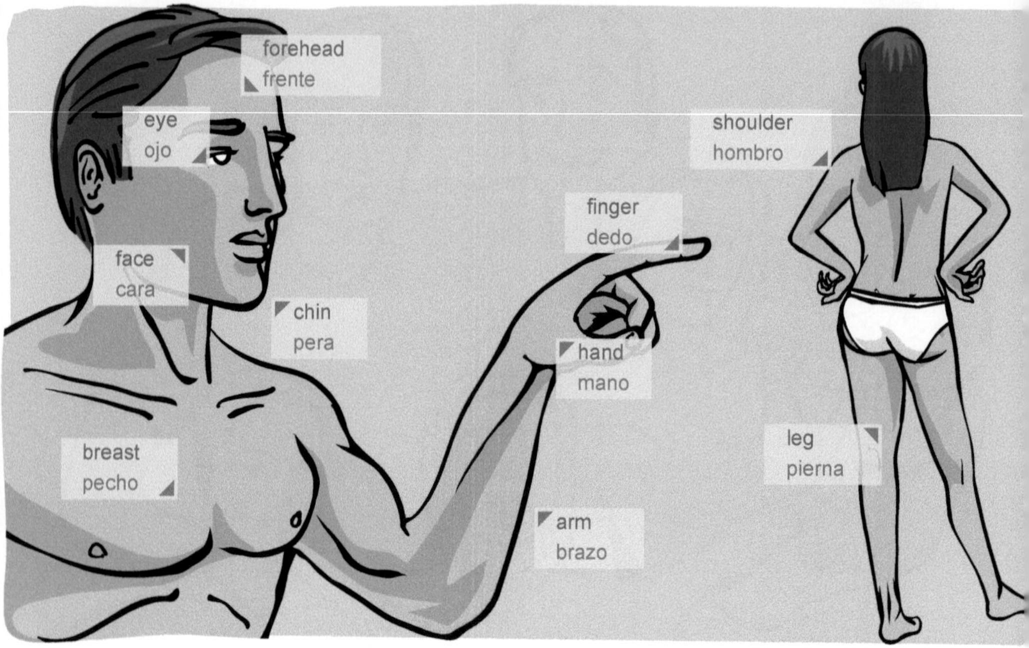

forehead
frente

eye
ojo

shoulder
hombro

finger
dedo

face
cara

chin
pera

hand
mano

breast
pecho

leg
pierna

arm
brazo

baby

bebé

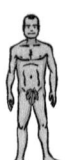

man

hombre

woman

mujer

girl

nena

boy

nene

head

cabeza

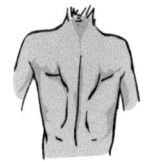

back

espalda

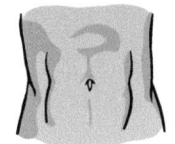

belly

panza

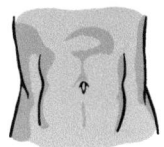

navel

ombligo

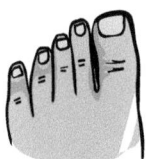

toe

dedo del pie

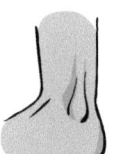

heel

talón

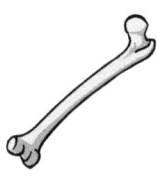

bone

hueso

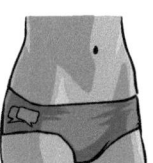

hip

cadera

knee

rodilla

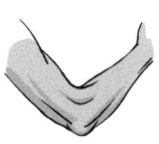

elbow

codo

nose

nariz

buttocks

cola

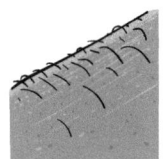

skin

piel

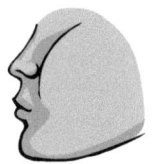

cheek

cachete

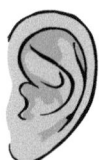

ear

oreja

lip

labio

body - cuerpo

mouth

boca

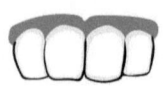

tooth

diente

tongue

lengua

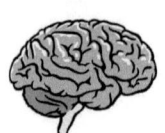

brain

cerebro

heart

corazón

muscle

músculo

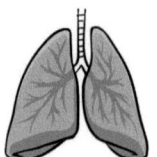

lung

pulmón

liver

hígado

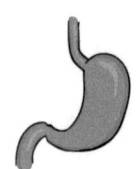

stomach

estómago

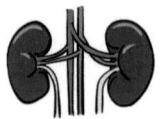

kidneys

riñones

sex

sexo

condom

preservativo

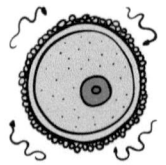

ovum

óvulo

semen

semen

pregnancy

embarazo

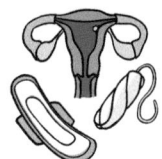

menstruation

menstruación

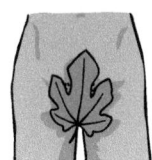

vagina

vagina

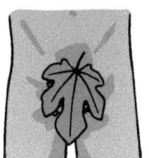

penis

pene

eyebrow

ceja

hair

pelo

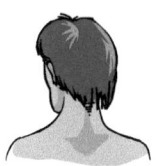

neck

cuello

hospital

hospital

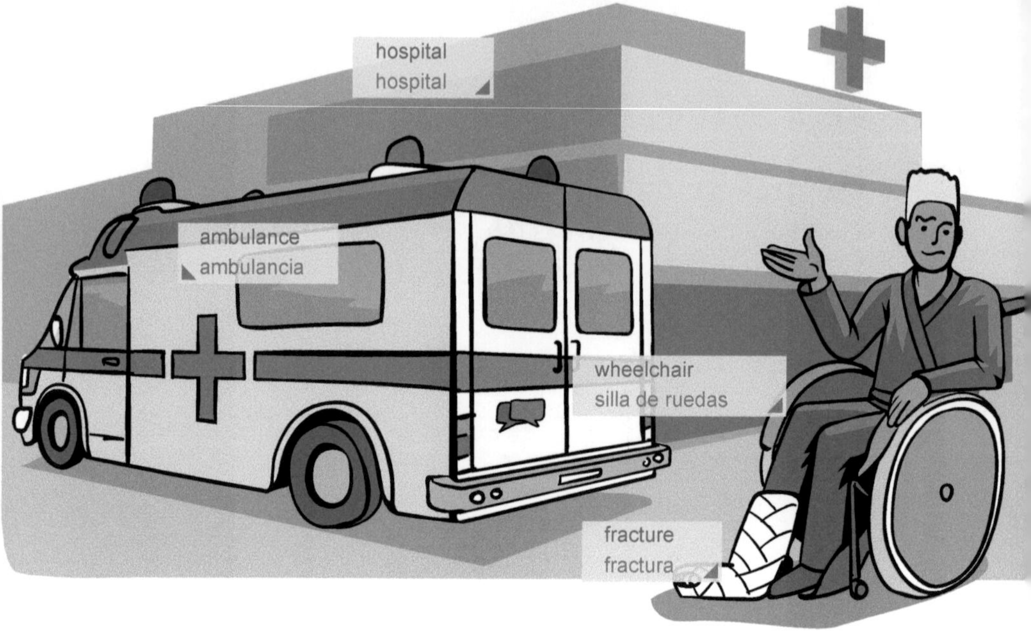

hospital
hospital
ambulance
ambulancia
wheelchair
silla de ruedas
fracture
fractura

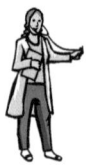

doctor

médico

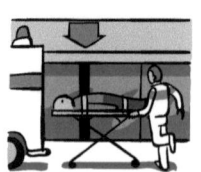

emergency room

sala de guardia

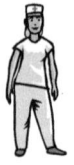

nurse

enfermera

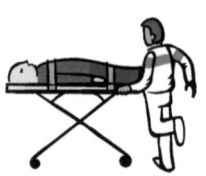

emergency

emergencia

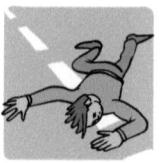

unconscious

inconsciente

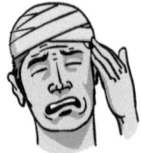

pain

dolor

injury

lesión

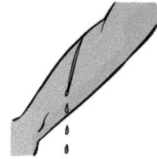

bleeding

hemorragia

heart attack

infarto

stroke

ACV

allergy

alergia

cough

tos

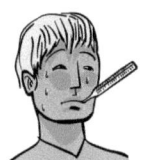

fever

fiebre

flu

gripe

diarrhea

diarrea

headache

dolor de cabeza

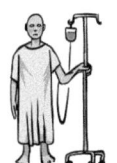

cancer

cáncer

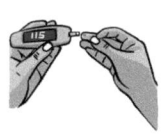

diabetes

diabetes

surgeon

cirujano

scalpel

bisturí

operation

operación

CT
TC

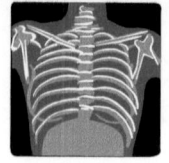

x-ray
rayos x

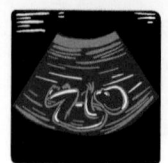

ultrasound
ecografía

face mask
barbijo

disease
enfermedad

waiting room
sala de espera

crutch
muleta

plaster
curita

bandage
venda

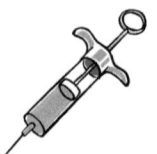

injection
inyección

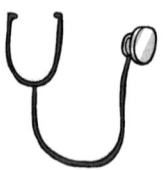

stethoscope
estetoscopio

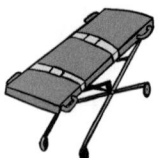

stretcher
camilla

clinical thermometer
termómetro

birth
nacimiento

overweight
sobrepeso

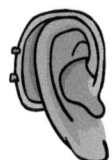

hearing aid

audífono

disinfectant

desinfectante

infection

infección

virus

virus

HIV / AIDS

VIH / SIDA

medicine

remedio

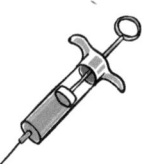

vaccination

vacunación

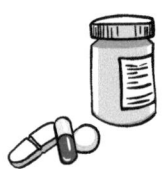

tablets

comprimidos

pill

pastilla anticonceptiva

emergency call

llamada de emergencia

blood pressure monitor

tensiómetro

ill / healthy

enfermo / sano

Help!
¡Ayuda!

alarm
alarma

assault
agresión

attack
ataque

danger
peligro

emergency exit
salida de emergencia

Fire!
¡Fuego!

fire extinguisher
matafuego

accident
accidente

first-aid kit
botiquín de primeros
auxilios

SOS
SOS

police
policía

Europe

Europa

North America

América del Norte

South America

América del Sur

Africa

África

Asia

Asia

Australia

Australia

Atlantic

Atlántico

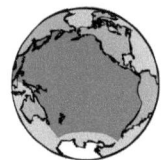

Pacific

Pacífico

Indian Ocean

Océano Índico

Antarctic Ocean

Océano Antártico

Arctic Ocean

Océano Ártico

North pole

polo norte

South pole

polo sur

Antarctica

Antártida

earth

Tierra

land

tierra

sea

mar

island

isla

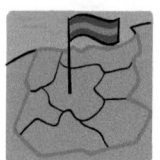

nation

nación

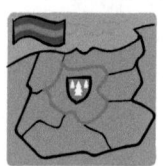

state

estado

clock face

esfera

hour hand

manecilla de las horas

minute hand

minutero

second hand

segundero

What time is it?

¿Qué hora es?

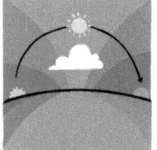

day

día

time

hora

now

ahora

digital watch

reloj digital

minute

minuto

hour

hora

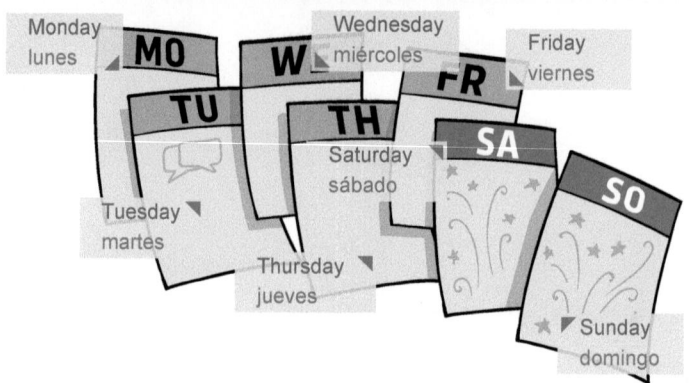

Monday — lunes
Wednesday — miércoles
Friday — viernes
Tuesday — martes
Saturday — sábado
Thursday — jueves
Sunday — domingo

yesterday

ayer

today

hoy

tomorrow

mañana

morning

mañana

noon

mediodía

evening

tarde

workdays

días hábiles

weekend

fin de semana

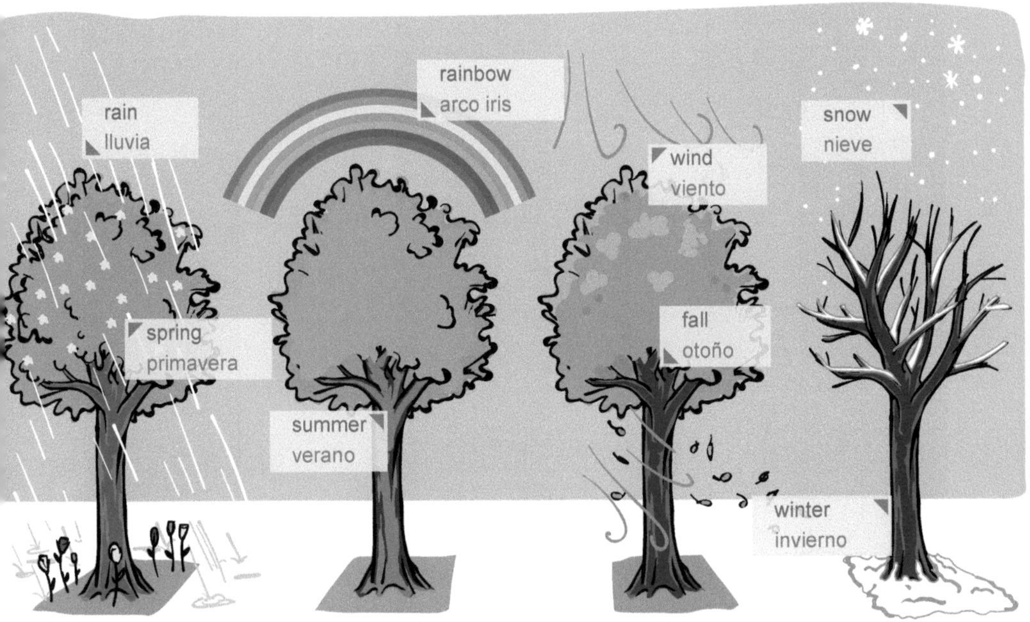

rain
lluvia

rainbow
arco iris

wind
viento

snow
nieve

spring
primavera

summer
verano

fall
otoño

winter
invierno

4.APRIL	11°	
5.APRIL	4°	
6.APRIL	13°	
7.APRIL	8°	
8.APRIL	10°	

weather forecast

pronóstico meteorológico

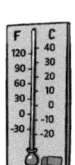

thermometer

termómetro

sunshine

luz del sol

cloud

nube

fog

niebla

humidity

humedad

lightning

rayo

thunder

trueno

storm

tormenta

hail

granizo

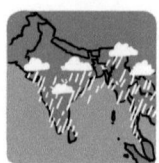

monsoon

monzón

flood

inundación

ice

hielo

January

enero

February

febrero

March

marzo

April

abril

May

mayo

June

junio

July

julio

August

agosto

year - año

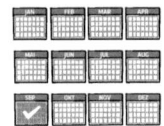

September
....
septiembre

October
....
octubre

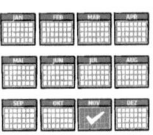

November
....
noviembre

December
....
diciembre

shapes
formas

circle
....
círculo

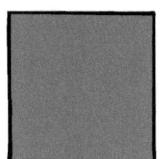

square
....
cuadrado

rectangle
....
rectángulo

triangle
....
triángulo

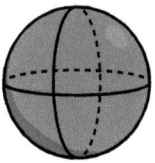

sphere
....
esfera

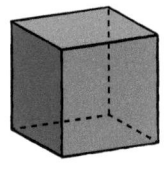

cube
....
cubo

colors

colores

white

blanco

yellow

amarillo

orange

naranja

pink

rosa

red

rojo

purple

violeta

blue

azul

green

verde

brown

marrón

gray

gris

black

negro

a lot / a little

mucho / poco

angry / calm

enojado / tranquilo

beautiful / ugly

lindo / feo

beginning / end

principio / fin

big / small

grande / chico

bright / dark

claro / oscuro

brother / sister

hermano / hermana

clean / dirty

limpio / sucio

complete / incomplete

completo / incompleto

day / night

día / noche

dead / alive

muerto / vivo

wide / narrow

ancho / angosto

edible / inedible

comestible / no comestible

evil / kind

malo / amable

excited / bored

entusiasmado / aburrido

fat / thin

gordo / flaco

first / last

primero / último

friend / enemy

amigo / enemigo

full / empty

lleno / vacío

hard / soft

duro / blando

heavy / light

pesado / liviano

hunger / thirst

hambre / sed

ill / healthy

enfermo / sano

illegal / legal

ilegal / legal

intelligent / stupid

inteligente / estúpido

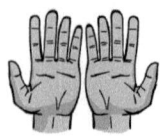

left / right

izquierda / derecha

near / far

cerca / lejos

new / used

nuevo / usado

nothing / something

nada / algo

old / young

viejo / joven

on / off

encendido / apagado

open / closed

abierto / cerrado

quiet / loud

silencioso / ruidoso

rich / poor

rico / pobre

right / wrong

correcto / incorrecto

rough / smooth

áspero / suave

sad / happy

triste / contento

short / long

corto / largo

slow / fast

lento / rápido

wet / dry

mojado / seco

warm / cool

caliente / frío

war / peace

guerra / paz

opposites - opuestos

0

zero

cero

1

one

uno

2

two

dos

3

three

tres

4

four

cuatro

5

five

cinco

6

six

seis

7

seven

siete

8

eight

ocho

9

nine

nueve

10

ten

diez

11

eleven

once

12
twelve

doce

13
thirteen

trece

14
fourteen

catorce

15
fifteen

quince

16
sixteen

dieciséis

17
seventeen

diecisiete

18
eighteen

dieciocho

19
nineteen

diecinueve

20
twenty

veinte

100
hundred

cien

1.000
thousand

mil

1.000.000
million

millón

English

inglés

American English

inglés americano

Chinese Mandarin

chino mandarín

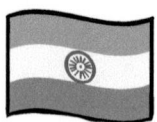

Hindi

hindi

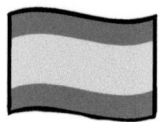

Spanish

español

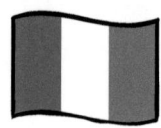

French

francés

Arabic

árabe

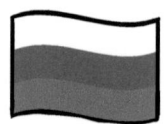

Russian

ruso

Portuguese

portugués

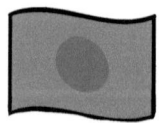

Bengali

bengalí

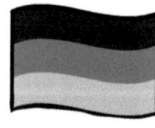

German

alemán

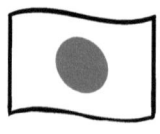

Japanese

japonés

I

yo

you

vos

he / she / it

él / ella

we

nosotros

you

ustedes

they

ellos

who?

¿quién?

what?

¿qué?

how?

¿cómo?

where?

¿dónde?

when?

¿cuándo?

name

nombre

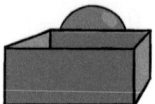

behind

detrás

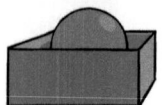

in

en

in front of

adelante de

over

por encima de

on

sobre

under

debajo de

beside

al lado de

between

entre

place

lugar